A Radiance
Like Wind or Water

Poems by Richard Ronan

Dragon Gate, Inc.
Port Townsend, Washington

Grateful acknowledgment is due to the editors of the fol-
lowing periodicals, where some of the poems in this vol-
ume first appeared: *American Poetry Review* ("A Sight-
ing of Whales" and "*Lachrymae Rerum*"); *Berkeley
Poetry Review* ("One Hundred Aspects of the Moon,"
"The Idea of Twins," "Haiku and Lyric," "Towards
Sleep" and "Horizontal"); *Northwest Review* ("July/
Here"); *Poetry Northwest* ("Pine/Eucalyptus/Fennel");
and *Telescope* ("Sleepwalk Watercolor" and "Lady in a
Northern Province").

ISBN 0-937872-14-8
ISBN 0-937872-15-6 (paperback)
Library of Congress #83-72376

First Printing
9 8 7 6 5 4 3 2

Published by Dragon Gate, Inc., 508 Lincoln Street, Port
Townsend, Washington 98368.

for W.S.P.—tat tvam asi

�֍

"*Yanks at* Chadō" *is for Denise*

"*Haiku and Lyric*" *is for Jane*

"Die Kunst der Fuge" *is for Gwen*

"A *Sighting of Whales*" *is for Terri*

❋ Contents

The relation between pain and beauty is the major problem ... felt at all stages and degrees. But *in the insolubility of the problem lies the meaning.* ... It is answered by being stated. All solutions are false. ... Only the question, the dilemma, the contradiction is true and eternally valid. Our desire to live ... more abundantly—this is the essence.

R. H. Blythe, *Haiku*, Volume 2: Spring.
(Hokuseido Press, Tokyo, 1981.)

Mondō

—Sensei, how are we to know,
while there is sorrow in the world
and while we live in the world of sorrow?

—By a slow or sudden falling away of the sorrow,
like rain, by a gradual or abrupt forgetting to doubt,
by a radiance simple as wind or water.

A Radiance
Like Wind or Water

❋ A Lady in a Northern Province

Colorless morning:
        my sleeves are weighted
with waxlike creatures of ice
            —fish, dogs, a white-
            blooded deer—

a thin winter,
        wide with your absence.

I have a carp frozen
        in a wheel of clear ice,
its orange veils of fire open,
its gold eyes wet and hard;
           for two days
        it has stood on a tile
        before my pallet,
           unmelting.

Yes, I love you most in this trial
           of winter;
love you also when the white goat
           looks at me
with sudden intelligence, compassion.
I love you at the pool's edge
        that bears in frosted mud
        the print of your feet,
           your palm, your hip.

In your absence
I've built a tight fire

which burns like the black wheel
in a tiger's eye.
I feed it coal
I feed it my hair, strand by strand,
so that you return whole
and undamaged
bearing a heart that is still mine.

✳ *A Lady in a Western Province*

Here flamingos gather
      to feed
   in their flight across-land.
They eat only things which are red:
         berries, ironstones.
They drink from each other,
     one upside down, the other bent
        in pity.

And the wrens also
fall here like hail,
      and the egrets who leave
      fish spines across the yard
      and white cuttle feathers.
Each species
passes my roof, touches
     my porch in weariness,
the order the same as last year's
     but no bird ever
     the same bird.

As your wife, I live here
    where the sun lodges,
      a host in your stead;
   where it alights briefly
      to cool itself
      between my breasts,
these ewes who were born in snow.

I know so little
   of what I do in a day

or of you, eternally walking
                your sword.
You tell me it is as it is,
                is as it must be; perhaps.
Yet no bird nests here, nor lingers;
            no line—not roof, nor fence-line,
            not the horizon itself—
                    is given the oval mystery
                    of an egg.

The sex over and done, we were, more or less,
      a charcoal ladder
        of coals.
When the breeze blew, his back glimmered up,
an orange rash of stars,
        mean-eyed in the dark,
      a thousand cats awakened in the future
      by the slit-eyed scent of rain.

We'd come to the cliffs again,
        leapt at each other's thighs
      and, in free fall, infinite and deep fall,
      committed again our infinite disregard
        for living long.
      Bones rung, singing like hammerheads
      struck on pads, muscle
            harder than bone,
      on skin stuck with the garment of tongues
          and juices.

And this time we broke the face
        of that wall of friends within,
      so fearful of our well-being,
        our audience of aunts;
he chewed my hard nipples raw,
      splintered a hip
        climbing on, in and out of me.
Then it went quick past pain,
      the fast male rush at the white circle
where pain lays out her silks
to be stolen or stained;

then this
                long, long apocalypse
        where I'm wondering wide, wondering down:
                how could I have opened his back
        like that with my fingers,
                so that it looks like a bird
                had dug there, a dog
        after the ass-end scent of his heart,
                and not have *known* it,
                neither he nor I,
so seized or suspended were we, so fire-mouthed.

Before he fell asleep between my legs,
                and became this impossible weight
        pulled by some magnet whose line runs from his thick body
                through mine to the center of a molten earth,
                        he said to my belly
                        that he'd kept cats
                        as a boy
                in milk boxes, a dovecote, bags sometimes;

        that he and his dimwit brother hunted them,
        lured them with cream and slabs of fish
        and then put them inside
        where they went wild with gut yowling
                and vicious hisses,

just to see them change, hear them change
from slow paws and pussies to a knot of claws
                and piss-white hatred,
        to sit quite close beside them while they tried
        to cut out his eyes,
                        to soft-talk them
                        some sweet trash and tell them
                        that he loved them.

❋ Heartwood

> The giant sequoias are subject to fires
> which leave large hollowed trunks scat-
> tered throughout the grove. Often the
> fired trees do not die, but continue to
> grow around and above the openings.
> These are sometimes as large as small
> caves.

Outside: redwood wall.
Lichen. Rich moss. The creaking quiet of the grove.
In: an irregular bricking of carbon,
scar-like, birth-stretched,
smelling of the wetness
of a long since gutted flame.
Outside: the live tree growing up
around this ashen pit
as if it stood spread-legged at its own pool's edge
avoiding its own pooled pain. Inside: open pith
whose absence
is this cavelet, lightless as a bed,
gained by low wound above a root-knob.
Only few have known it; entered.
We have known it.
Knotted shadows,
we are in it; have crawled through charcoal,
faces in the moss, left clothes in knots.

Quiet afternoon.
Birds. Wind creaking the needled tops,
the creaking deep and terrible inside.
We are nudes, white, blind,
blackened in patches from the burnt oxbow
we've bowed beneath,

from black walls we've rubbed.
Here
in the belly of the god,
eating each other's mouths, throats.
Birds go away. The wind spirals inside above us,
slow water in a drain.
Wet-smeared mud on the hair-ring of nipples,
pocked cinders in the smooth rounds of butt
and muscle,
you standing, an arm taut as green wood,
a leg, pushing in each direction
against the black wood-ring
a mouth   maybe mine
mouths your legs, the dark musk between
tasting of ash and pineseed;
                              licks your wrists,
paste of redwood grit, saliva, sweat
and tongue.

            Lightless afternoon.
Denim shorts balled up with socks, gray, woolen,
hiker's boots, khaki pack, felt not seen
eyes in the dark
white gism flung across space   a ghost penis
chests heaving with luminous hair.
I feel a nest, a bone,
my back to the black loam, your breath
above, hard, as if in storm.
I am sinking my fingers
into the redwood soot floor,
touching the place
from which the root grows down.

✳ *Egret/Heron/Redwood/Light*

The herons come first,
in winter, at the beginning of the year,
blue-gray and weathered like wood,
to remake the bony nests which the winter rains
have loosened,
to eat the tops of the redwoods
into a great basin
that has widened over a century into arms,
into one upswept embrace.

Then the white egrets come, inherit the well-worked nests,
the flattened blue trees.
They descend as white rain, like the whole
simplicity of the Orient,
long-legged aerial dancers, back-fanning,
cooling the branches they barely move
as they touch them,
the egrets who lay thin miraculous feathers
on the branches,
the egrets who stand as if in flight,
still and in couples,
indicating the way toward light
to their furred chicks.

We watch them from the mountain lookout,
my lover, my great friend and I,
three columns of light,
arrayed like white Greeks
on a cypress stage
which may be the world,
standing lights obscured by shadow and
forgetfulness,

sometimes brought out by birds
and passage
to see ourselves transfigured,
lovely among blue-green trees,
many thousand bees making a single hum
around a flowering shrub
in the heat and stillness of place.

❋ *Photograph*

There is a photograph in my mind's eye
of the day we went to the mountain.
There is the gold-straw valley in it,
the crude, exquisite pine,
the mineral brook coming from
a stand of rock,
seeping into a pool,
enlivening an oval shore of watercress,
then
a thin tail of the same pepper-green
that trails down the closed valley
to the steep mountain ledge, then
the ravine, the deep throat of which
is thick with mist
and beneath which is the inlet
of the western ocean.

We are kissing, I above you somewhat
on a breadloaf of stone,
your head angled back, as if in a faint,
a melt.
I have drunk a mouthful of the brookwater
and as I kiss you I am dribbling
its cold metal shock into your throat.
I am myself made fluid by this,
am running, turning inside out,
down this rope of water as it twists
into you from my mouth,
from the stone-cleft brook,
from the lost heart where water's
first born.

In the photograph we can see
this happen;
see ourselves overlap and ebb between
each other's mouths;
see ourselves spilling with the pondweed
and watercress,
here, kissing, standing in twilight,
and there, also, below the mist,
you and I, yes, a stain of green-gold ice
entering the sea.

✳ *Yanks at* Chadō

We are on high ground, like long-legged birds
above tree top, the view wide, far,
banked by dark leaves.
The glass wall reveals the sun, centered
at eye-level, like a brother;
reveals, too, the ongoing influx of fog,
a wall itself, but lower, quite far below us
—a white wall, as is the yellow light a wall,
brittle, commingled with the effacing water
of the bay, the wet, beaded air.

We kneel in long, separate shadows, in the glare:
the rug made colorless,
the vase of tiny roses black in silhouette.
She turns the cup for us, passes it.
Foam settles in the tea.
We admire the glaze, the river of light
rising to flood.
We are kneeling in a row, in the silence of friends,
sudden, inevitable, arranged in
the long narrow corridor we make of ourselves.
We aspire to politeness, care, attention.
She aspires to the freedoms of ritual.
And each is a master
without effort or justice
solely by virtue of our talent to be
caught by light, in silence.
The wooden scent of green tea,

the minute hiss of its bubbles breaking away.
The weave in the rug, the warp of time, the light
warm on our faces
as we bow in thanks for meagerness.
We are here perfectly, in peace,
brilliant within, among friends.

✳ Die Kunst der Fuge

*Bach's "Art of Fugue" is not specified
for instrumentation. It is a study in
form without regard to the real effect
of which instrument is to play which
part. It is pure in this sense, form
existing in an ideal, unheard sphere.
It has any number of times been
orchestrated for concert as Bach might
have done it, but of course did not.*

Fugue statement, variation:
this is the inner music, our working all night
with one to find the other, sweating, systole,
diastole, lung contracting
to expand in sweat, our falling together
from the mattress onto the wood floor, record skipping
and there is no light.
        Only in discovery
is there newness in us, all else dies as it's heard,
is not music, does not renew.

*

The fugue options, though nearly infinite,
are not infinite, the patterns,
patchworked mirrors and ornamenting
that enter and attach, though nearly infinite,
are not infinite; are set. Sad
at first to be a thing in time and know;
joyous at last.
The swan is dying eternally
in the Children's Pond, tapping
its sad, red beak on a basswood trunk,
floating dead with the ripples of pondwater.

Every swan dies and there is only one swan;
also, there are many—each swan that lives—
and in the workings of these two themes
is bleak beauty, joy, loss and music.

*

First silence—
              you know in your best
moments that realization is profounder than belief;

then music—
              that in making *sense, rather*
than in *sense, we renew,*
spider spinning, inventing the inevitable
as it falls across the window.

Then silence and music interpenetrated—
              sword blade run through the blade of a knife,
              two rivers at the mixed mouth of the sea.
              It is the third water
              which we now hear.

*

Not this which is heard, not fact, the *it* itself, no,
it is not sufficient before its own import,
the intimate passenger in it, of it, forming
the fugue which is already formed.
                              We are sleeping now,
linens like rope, breathing, two breathings.

              It is January in the music.
              The heart of a bear inside the heartwood of a tree
              is beating at its winter rate,

the something-else is sounding,
overtones,
in the lungs, resonant, murmuring:
this
is one of the shapes which were infinite.

Let us worship in sweat and love the shapes,
for at last they are few, they are precious,
and we are falling,
brief as music.

❋ *January*

The dawn:
window glass iced over,
a composition of block and sparks,
sunlight, thin, involuting in hazed crystal.
The rhododendron leaves collapsed
into dry leather: it's bitter cold.
The smoke, unmoving, trim and concise,
vertical, tensed:
                    the quite early morning.
We are awake, not-speaking,
at home with sensing that which is exquisite
—the frost landscape,
the lush life we jointly live—
with the awed uselessness of the exquisite,
the purposeless point of seeing/being
that cargo of pattern and pointless sense
            which arrives like this,
                    revealed, silent,
in early winter before we're too exhausted,
still naïve,
quiet and able to listen:
                    listening ice ringing in the hard sun
                    listening pine separating the wind
                            with a thin broom of fingers.
The breaths are heard,
the two hearts in coverlets are heard,
the twickings of the eye
            looking up at one thing alone is heard:
                    the numberless suns that rise over
each of our lives, milk-moist, milk-white, clear
            as water in our mouths
are heard in their silence.

❋ Doing Dishes

> To know pine, go to the pine;
> bamboo to the bamboo.
> Leave behind this clinging to yourself.
> You will only impose and never learn.
> —Bashō

A round blue-winged bird
    spattering the puddle at the dip in the drive.
Above,
    the broom hedge spilling yellow in fat heaps
    and over this, the red bridge hung in the gap
of hills losing themselves in themselves,
    mounded cloud crossing clean above these,
    like the same thought perfected
        and sent east.

And the scent of a sweet small flower,
silent, hid
waving under a wide shrub's hem
or indistinct beneath a fence: it fills us.

Billy, you know,
    it *is* in witnessing, in watching;
    it is in this staring through the glass
        at the yard with the hands soaped
    and holding a light plate,
        that it seems to have a sense,
    an order, a fineness of its own
        to which we've been invited.

On the one hill is the heart; the other the mind

and there is a bridge between
    and a bird blue as blood

and a pride of cloud roaring
       its head of news backwards across
the country to the places where we were born.

I think it's good, you know,
I think it's growing upon us like the colored dawn.

✳ Soe

You step from the shower,
the water beaded,
worked into ringlets down a tight
oiled skin: our lives
are running beside each other
like vines climbing themselves,
reaching up the bed,
beneath the breakfast table,
shared hands/mouth/hair.
There is a rooted part of us.
We are an event continuing
before our own eyes.

I think of gods
because of you,
now standing in the doorway,
lighted by white walls and dampness:
I think that they are beautiful, of course,
skins like dolphins or seals spinning
through water—
and that they are flesh,
that they live only as flesh,
among us, as us,
every morning rubbing the steam
from the mirror in the bathroom,
squinting at their jaws:
gods.

Soe: it means the place of man
in the line from earth to heaven;
also, the purpose of a man:

to be the eyes and ears of heaven,
the blood of earth, mouth of god, the flesh
shining before a speechless tongue
of clay.
It is today your task to arrive, moist,
tossing rain like a terrier;
mine to see it occur
in our tangle of time,
to say that it is here,
now, like this.

All day long I write this,
drinking the thin waters
that gather on your spine,
mouth of god, tongue of man.

❋ Haiku and Lyric

bamboo/layer-burdened/shells of ice
bird blood red/water-water/thornflower
winter/future early/here

*

The bamboo windbreak bows with ice.
A male cardinal bright as blood
twists a nutseed, rides the rise and fall
of a rose branch.
Everywhere the snowscape spans outward
toward the city, toward the empty west
upward into gray, inward.
All is feeling, obscure, mixed, unlike
the single bird defining the world of whites
and shadow-whites, knowing itself, utterly.

*

bamboo blurred with ice
grayed sky, numb, deafened by snow
a redbird burning

❈ *Loft Bed*

Lying in the corners of the bed, in shapes shaped
    like letters, brush marks for words like:
        nazuna, ba, mireba, kana,
    linking, overlapping, referring again
to every other night when we've made love,
    like this or in some other language:
        here, we are here; or
this, this, written and writing all night
        on the white sheet
        in darkness
    precious in time; lost in time
still   smile   tears   again   here

＊

the camellias are
        in bloom at home
in the terrible green
        weather of midwinter
whorled rosettes
        in the fog
rouge, rose, cameo-gray

❋ *Despair before Spring*

Nearly March.
The veined head of maple reddens,
the hair of the willow yellows to the tips;
saps rise,
the turning from winter
that the planet's habit has made inevitable.

Faith of fact—
we seek it, hungering connection,
the knowing of being.
                        Nearly March,
and the days in the calendar
are windowed, looking outside season
and habit
into the unadorned, wild air of saints,
the nude landscape the soul
carries from the first truly
and stands with at its end,
truly saying: *This is so,*
and we are this—
armload of pussy willow,
forsythia, shield of fruiting moss.
It is congruence we count,
the mirror-days when both calendars
catch each other passing,
the juncture in the planet's turning
where the daily joins
the eye of god.

Nearly March.
Says Senno:
The moment-before,
not the moment-of
is perfectest beauty,
the unopened iris, the just-coloring bud.
And the long days, the vast year ungiving
before the turning,
says St. John,
is our fast of abandonment,
our meaningless endurance.
Nearly March,
full of hunger, longing
for alignment with a faith,
we try to keep a budded rose
burning in the wet lamp.

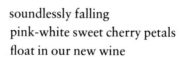

soundlessly falling
pink-white sweet cherry petals
float in our new wine

❊ Sleepwalk Watercolor

By recall alone we know
    the pale block of butter
    square
    on the violet plate;
sense the charcoal smear across
    an oyster sky:
    clouds   jet streams   red tower lights
pointing themselves out in series
    going bottom/low/up/midway/high/away/blind:
the skyscape blurred with dark edging and remnant light—
    the night/the world/the other,
    outside as dark as in.

There are two apples on the sill
    a yam rooting in a glass
    three tomatoes softly red
    peaches colored in sunset
    '   and half colors
    each sitting in sugar
    winding water in the dark.
There are boats on the bay, unseen,
    that take the mind away.
There are houses everywhere
    where our future waits,
    staring from a rear window at a bridge.
There is a longing that occurs
    like a walking not brought fully out of sleep
    a longing constructing events,

reciting the days,
placing the furniture,
an aching to be some place utterly
and not to be entrapped there:
to be nowhere
everywhere ghostlike
in the lap of god.

✳

thunder rolls through snow
an instant of lightning
snow/sky/earth
        pure light

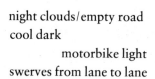

night clouds/empty road
cool dark
            motorbike light
swerves from lane to lane

✳ Soft Speed

Sixty sixty-five:
wind's roar warm
early summer
countless insects, grains
of pollen, seeds,
the debris of the June air
streaking past
splattering sometimes
wet on the windshield,
infinite
yellow points—
seven miles of buttercups
pulling into soft lines,
soft lines into
a vapor of honeysuckle
whose coming and going
cannot be told.
Coming it is
the scent of the vine,
then the remembrance
of the scent;
gone it is the moment
of honeysuckle isolated
somewhere
like a gateway
through which we pass.

tiger lilies lean
sunward from a slag of coal
noon/exhaust fumes/sun

❋ *July/Here*

We lie on the roof.
A flight of birds converging for a moment
into an off-center swirl, an arabesque above us.
We stare up at it and at the neuter sky,
the flight in phosphorus left glittering
on the plate of the eye,
a message in cursive form that destructs
in revelation.

I am sick with thinking of how to live and where
and what it costs to do it and if any of it is truly wise;
sick thinking of my mad mother wringing her hands
in a house south of here,
my sister realizing all at once a lifetime of rage,
their circular stairwell of grief and how we cannot
seem to get to the upper storey,
all the while knowing that peace is on the upper storey
awaiting us; thought-sick that it's again
a Jersey summer, wet, blistering sunlight
surrounding every breath, the plants steaming
in their wet beds.
I say to myself that I need a drink of water.

My lover watches the birds, thinking of the childhood
south of summers, oleander and August murders,
and also of the coolness of the northwest
at this same time of year;
of jobs and time and brothers and sex and the northeast,
here, where we somehow have gotten,
in this heat bath of smog, this stillness of not-raining,
and says: A drink of water would be nice.

I break the ice apart into our glasses,
then place one chunk to the place between my eyes.
For a moment it grows dark and I am drawing
a word on the hot roof
with the wet ice. The birds are gone.
It is July here in this place,
this,
my mother's country,
my sister's house.

❋ *Spring into Summer*

Looking up at a green sky
at the crest of thunderstorm
many winged pods of maple
twisting across everywhere
in currents and gusts
upward, down.
The setter, chin down on a dry island
of her own shape
isolated hard beads of rain
falling straight onto her head.
Lightning brightens her tongue, her eyes
then downpour
the hose lost in a two-inch lake
the sound of stone tearing open
in the sky,
drowning ants
a black lace on the surface
of the water.

❋ Horizontal

Blue scrim   skin before skin
of round hills   above around upon
the lake-like bay   skein of high cloud
         warp of long cloud
         flume of fog moving in relentless for the interior.

Twin birds crossing between the slung roadway
      of the bridge from west to east,
a cool wind oblique from the northwest
      upon their feathered cheeks.

The red dog pushing his nose through leaves,
      hunting the scent of geography
         and you, my hand, your hand and I,
      walking sidewise on the street
         to buy groceries and bleach,
         in love with what passes in a day,
      through a life, two lives engaged as one life,
         satisfied and knowing better.

Oh the days, the days as they come
like gifts on the morning porch, speaking
      in dry dirt and high humidity,
      in weather and circumstance;
how we walk through the blue days
         with few others—
      sweaters, shoes, books and tables,
      cold tea, clock in our mouths.

mulberries fallen
purple concrete black jelly
swarming dark ants

✳ The Idea of Twins

Blackbirds opening their planked wings
in the oaks which now in autumn
are cinnabar and burning,
drunk on their own unstable sugar.
The weather hung across the Sound,
it walls the overhead, a ceiling of stones
like a fireplace wall.
We fear the future that hangs beyond this,
the white light higher than white light.
Below, we are moody and split hairs,
infinitives, wood for the fireplace,
tomorrow uncertain.

When I arrange the field orchis
in the round shell we've taken off the beach
I think
that the future is what we say
when we mean
the great way that things simply are;
and that this never lives at quiet ease
with the things that compose it and aspire
toward it,
the things lying flatwise on the beach
—nor with *us*, wet-footed among these shells.
It is what we say when we mean
that above the roof-dome of rock-cloud
there is a white bird which is the meaning
of the crow,

ever opening its feathers across its own eye of light,
the bird who smiles,
the unseen gestures of a bird
in a shadow of something birdlike here,
which we see, now, in autumn,
in its black form
from out the corner of our worldly eye.

❋ *Poor Flesh*

The astonishing fluorescence of this autumn
in which, an hour and a half south of here,
my father lies dying: the gold
on yellow, yellow on peach,
the red blotted through green.

Here, a berry vine, blood and coral red,
the tree it climbs, a pale blue spruce;
here, a blue aster, small
beneath a vermilion hood of sumac.

The light falls thinner, at a low angle.
Cooling air. The departure of birds.
The beautiful and sad
seem forever mixed in us.
We are their ground, they our climate and season.

This is our theme.

*

The drive is from the industrial North,
our pie-slice of the chemical ring
that surrounds the city,
to the flat south
of inland marsh and shoreline.
It is nearly two hours each way;
in the fall, it is a colorful drive,
if a long one in feeling: Rutherford,
Bloomfield, Montclair, Orange, Vaux Hall,
Kenilworth, Atlantic City, Tom's River.

By these the autumn moves southward
down the parkway
from suburban riot to the oxblood and scrub pine
of the southern part of the state.
We move down time;
drive back, up to the present,
weekly, sometimes daily, if he has turned
for the worse—
                    time, place, the connection of towns,
their endless nonconnection to each other
or to the road. The soul
is said to be playful with such things
—time, place, our poor realm of pity—
and cruel to the body
when the body has been deaf to it.
A terrible wife, the soul of a man,
but a faithful one.

To think of this in autumn
is to strive to allow it;
to think of this in transit
is a way, I know, toward surrender
to the man's death.

... And it may be pointless: he, his life,
our efforts now, nice accommodations to the inevitable.
No, it *is* pointless; at least cruel
to our notion of point,
steadfast only to its own pointed design
which eludes us.

Prayer on the highway: *Oh God,*
let the design

inform us gently;
oh let us see it, at last,
as beautiful.

*

My father was first stricken by cancer of
the colon, having witnessed his own father
and uncle succumb slowly to cancers of the
jaw. His colon was removed, a colostomic
device inserted through his intestines.
Soon after, his sister and younger brother
both fell victim to the same disease and
treatment. Within a year, my father's
cancer had metastasized to his thighbone,
which quickly eroded. Just before Christ-
mas, he collapsed trying to get up the
cellar steps: the bone quite simply fell
apart. An aluminum rod was implanted in
his leg and he lived in hope that he would,
as a result, be again able to walk; he was
not. For awhile, with the aid of a metal
walker, he could pull himself painfully
from bed to table to chair, but as the can-
cer spread through his bones to his chest
and hip, he was unable to support his own
weight even with the aid of these metal
devices. His final hospitalization lasted
about three months, from early autumn to
winter. During this period I, my brother,
mother and sister commuted separately from
our various places in the state to the
place of his confinement. For most of this
time, he was sedated by a combination of

morphine and Valium. He spoke seldom, and
then out of a drug-induced haze.

He died at the end of November.

*

We drive:
a roof of birds overhead and to the west
in thousand lots; they migrate with us,
the road turning under them,
until, in a gesture, a vast aerial wave,
they veer, drop all together into the low marsh.

This part of the state is set aside
for their travel, and thus, their kind:
a mud estuary of soft channels,
snaking herds of frail pampas grass
which surrender like a single thing
to breezes.
There was once a swamp cedar
or clump-birch indigenous to this barren;
also a kind of muskrat
found nowhere else; now both found nowhere
at all.
Now there are only birds,
these brown citizens of two climates;
sometimes large geese, also ducks
of several sorts.

A wind blows a rush of leaves upwards.
The sparrows, who do not leave us,
also rush up with these, frightened.
Together leaves and birds ride the currents,
then abruptly fall back into grass.

*

Several times
we were called,
told he would not
survive the night.
By several routes
we rushed south
and sat the night
sleepless
beside the bed.
These several times
he endured, heaving,
gripping the metal
bed-rails, trying to rise,
saying Oooohh;
but each night
survived
only made the next
more final: we stayed.
At last, in shifts,
we sat a deathwatch,
two weeks, three,
a month, five weeks,
six.

*

The lesser roads off the highway
are gorgeous arcades of yellow,
raining, thick, wine-scented,
reminiscent of the first impact of spring.

The light, however, is not the same light,
there, at the end of the street

like a beacon seen from a yellow sea,
the street where the whole world
is burning.

This is the transformation of sorrow, burning
in the distance; the meaning in death,
like the meaning in fire,
fire in the eyes trying to die,
eyes in the sea of fever,
the fever gathering snow.

In his body my father's soul is burning,
as if the body were a smooth thin tree,
like a birch, or a beech perhaps,
and the red spirit, a fountain of wild grape,
enflamed in October,
supported by the gray wood,
but wholly of another order.

Poor flesh,
to be the host, the flammable witness,
the crux where such fire dances up itself
to brilliance and ash,
to a winter and irrelevance of flesh,
an unplace about which
we've only the split bones of guesswork
given down by next of kin.

All burn, Papa; some know they burn.
Few know the wheel that steers the flame.

        *

You are breathing like a fish.
My brother is sleeping under your bed,

twitching in his large body with dreams
of the Asian war: Death as an anaconda
nesting beneath his hooch. He is dreaming
of his friend whose head exploded.
The head spits out shrimps and Chinese
movie posters. It is a maw.
Death the god, the constant, the inevitable.
We all were raised with the head.
None of us danced.

. . . The sky is lightening.

Across the hall the madman
who may never die
is hopping on the same syllable:
Ha-ha-ha-ha-ha-ha.

Je ne fais jamais ah-ah-ah
said Fontenelle, dying, about laughing;
each syllable sounded to him too much
like the last.

      Maple

      oak

      birch

      beech

      dropping

      *

MORPHINE SULFATE
IN SODIUM SOLUTION
500 CC
BOTTLE #8

Trees colored now only by absence.

The leaves of deciduous trees gone now,
the pine seems to return to us,
though in truth it has only remained,
been revealed as the other greens fell away.

It is not unlike bone. Or spirit.

                    *

How can you die? How can death be?
How do we live in such suffering, like horses
pulling a sled of carrion and memory?
The earth is dead and there is no god left
to kiss us and our family is a map of scars,
your bones, your hollow bones winding down
the stairwell of grief to water and pulp.

We drive through red and orange tunnels,
the fields black in the distance.

                    *

... Anything that erodes the borders
of our smallness lets in something divine,
awesome, terrible, and itself small.

I dream of a plum tree,
its branch broken by a tubercular child.
She stands still in the sudden and enormous
context of the tree.

*

BOTTLE #9

*

I hold your cool hand as you pull
at the bed-rails. "There's a light coming
through the stairs," you tell me.
Yes, it's true,
                we are not made of time,
but light, Papa.
Death is not a kingdom sucking the living dry;
it is small and actual, with us, neuter,
faceless because it will not take the face
we offer it.
And the soul, the soul is the exact shape
of the body, a little cloud
with red eyes and nerves,
which is not subject to the things of time,
but subjects those things
to its inexplicable rough will. It does not
feel pain, only longing, longing sometimes
worse than pain.
Yes, I see it through the stairs; it's very bright,
don't be afraid, let neither of us be afraid.
Death.
We do not know what to say,

but know that we must witness it,
that we must witness each other,
that this will make enormous difference.

*

My brother is sleeping, falling now from the chair,
the TV flickering, soundless.
He is here lest you be as frightened as he was,
alone in the jungle, drugged,
in horror, watching the anaconda hatch its young
in his shoes, in his heart.

You open your eyes.
He wakens and takes your hand.
Your eyes are no longer glazed gray, but clear,
perfected.
You do not speak, but seem amazed,
yourself again and profoundly calm.
He holds your hand. You are alone together.
It is very quiet in the flickering light.
When you die, you do so gently
so that it does not frighten him.

*

Sunrise.
December.
Light breaking
on a shelf of glass: splotches, bars,
circlets, ten thousand flecks
pulled livid into spectrum across the kitchen.

Outside, late fall, the going-backwards,
the retracting from proliferation,

unstringing the light the leaf ate and became,
the light bred green,
the green bled red, salmon,
mauve.
　　　　Sugar is falling, the birch in flames.
We are climbing down the ladder
to a season of no color, time or heat,
the season where there is only
a wide snowfield and stillness,
ice glittering, sunlight.

Last night I felt that you came to me, Papa,
and we danced in each other's arms
like such good friends.

✽

tagged bird
bare moth
collide
over water

✳ Brown Moths

Dog-faced, hollow-faced, wood-faced,
fright-faced, oval-eyed and feathered
with fur   big moths of fat
cigar-stub bodies with clawed feet
like bicycle underparts;
and small moths, tear-shaped, small as wheat,
all powder and wings and hungry to be in
and burning on the bulb.

They return: this is pain
hung on a screen by night battering
the rusted web powdering the sill soot
left by rains that fell all spring
and do not fall in summer.
They are calling   the lane is calling
the eaves are calling, the sea, the entries of the sea,
the tide gates and each of the seasons are calling
and the call is like the inside meat
of the heart in the teeth of a dog
who's running off running down
the whole scheme of time:
the dog who never dies.

Buzzing anger, ellipses
around the ceiling fixture by two
who have come through, sick   dizzy
drunk   dying   they've come back
to drive at the heart   the call box
the humming transformer's red eye, the porch light,
any center   anything that makes the space
fall into shape.

Dog barks   dogs bark
he's turned the inside of my lip out
and sucked it into his mouth,
turned me into flesh, flesh hung like a ham in a cloud,
from a high roof-rafter of a high Swiss porch
on a mountain where the woods grow thin
and seem like death and god and the edge
of the rockbound world and nothing else.
And this is pain   betrayal, flesh and pain,
and he is pain and the door is pelting
with waddy thuds and soft talcy rage.

✳ One Hundred Aspects of the Moon

old
more leather thing than woman   I am old

how many moons crossing the sky
globes filling like breasts
half-bowls like breasts draining
one moon
always
within the ring of a hundred

my husband
my husband's sons

everywhere
paper pictures floating through pondwater
I sit breathing
the black stone at the bottom

moon above
moon on pond
a breeze
ten thousand shards of moon broken

breezeless   the moon   again
old at birth

❋ White Moths

When we see winter, we see a snow of moths
swept up across the bracken and the contracted field
of that place and this life;
the elm-tall sweep of these white insects,
as wide as clouds, the numberless civilization of them,
above the house, like a fire storm,
orbits up from a hollow hub
rages its soft maelstrom in silos,
in sea-heavy waves, in a spill that claws
at the sometimes glimpses of a lighted moon.

When we see the moon through cloud, we hear
the mixed voice, the two mouths
of sucking alternation and the unhungry still hub—
the sound of cold, hard light
pulling on the six-inch skin of water and ice,
of branch and cocoon: of moths
thick as air, white moths of every aspect,
weeping with and counter to god, in terror and brave,
narrating the spiral, the tidal upsweep
or else denying these.

When we see the world lifting like this,
when we feel our wet feet and our hair in contest
and the cold pelting of ice-spit and wings,
we are knowing something and denying it too,
our hours and the bones of the house
and the bones of each river which is uprooted and infected
with moon-pull and moth stillness;
we know winter   we know the life
in the house at the crossroads
upon and under storm landscape.

❋ Watching from the Headlands

Each earth surface a rich shelf of lives
        facing the sun
      and the hills here the color of light,
the color of a light which rises up from
the straw of harvest, a harvest in morning.

These grow on the meadow: salsify, thistle,
        sorrel, vetch;
     these on the porous sides of the cliffs
that drop yellow to the sea: tarweed, dudleya,
     sand verbena, sedum.

The tide moves through the body,
foot to cock to brain to eye.
We look to the headlands,
see green sea-hair carding without knot
in the coastal flux,
         seals sliding through.

This lesson: the edge of the sea, not the sea;
      not the vast tide, but the tide pool
        bearded in coral fan,
     sea slugs moving through, fluid knives
        slicing the small expanse,
    white anemone, barnacles spitting out
         feather lures for the small animals
        in the brine.

The surf slow, heavy against the vast shoulders
                of stone,
        the opulent thunder, white plinths of foam,
the liquid lead of seawater, the turquoise twisting
            into a fish well of it, an opal
                    opening downward into a sky-like blue.

❊ Lachrymae Rerum

On the mantel: coral, thin bones caught pink
in an old hand of water,
     a black lace of sea vegetable,
        two large shells of nautilus,
turning into center.
And on the table, forsythia made out to be a fountain
        spilling narcissus, wet leaf and rain.
Outside it rains,
        the soft impossible fall of droplets finer than air,
wetting the underside as fast as the face of things.
Our things. Ours as we are some other thing's.
Here in our home on its small earth,
        elements
     and the interspace resonant between.
You're sleeping, tears spilling
for no reasons except these:
the tears of things, the feeling that comprehension
is an exact and light sadness,
and that such sadness, such love,
such a place made up of our stark souvenirs and our selves,
if seen in truth, are finer than the stuff of which they are made.
        Damp ash in the fireplace
        papers across the kitchen table
        bed linens
        dark dishes without pattern,
            round, dull glazed,
          standing in the sink,
        your hair
        caught wet around your eyes.

❋ *Tea*

A fall showing of azalea, thin color,
pink where in spring it was a branch of redbirds.

Sparrows squat, dotting the tea stone white;
clouds broken, moving fast, blue between.

The maple red, a dried powder of blood.

Koi, motionless in the mouth of the clear stream
where it enters the pool, sunlight variable as sound upon them.

Cha is sadness, they say,
poverty, the gaunt autumn sun in warm patches
isolated in the cold shade:

One hand, a cup, the silence of attention,
the other hand saying, *By this, I show I live for you,*
for you, your air, a constancy, your earth ebbing
toward winter, waiting again to bear.

We are unable to hear the ring of the cup on the paper,
only half inclined to be here in utterness and to fall away
into this, into the vast coolness of which autumn
is but a gate,

able, unable, to go or return.

The roof of wisteria is yellow,
the leaves unsteady.

✳ Western Autumn

We drive the twisted road uphill
to the vista from which the bay, the city
are shown altogether. It seems
an infinitely round expanse.
We turn left, far left, winding the clay spool.
The earth is powder,
the roots driving deeper through shale,
the season sounding the high autumn shrill
of its last edge,
the honed, clear sound
after the hope of water
has been surrendered.
We stand together to watch the ellipse before us,
monumental steel and light,
the vast dry earth turning toward the east,
prostrate before the promise of winter.
We imagine
night here
or death/ecstasy/quietude
as a landscape
of minute lights beyond the high dark ledge
on which we stand,
green light, gold light, white,
the outlines of hills and inlets which comprise
the stillwater bay,
thin stars overhead in the mind,
as they are in the sky,
advancing towards a morning.
And our hearts are also hung.
We are the witnesses,
our view, a salt of light on darkness,
a reef of human tears.

✳ Fast—Fourth Day

The sky is rose, blue,
the deep, flat colors of hydrangea in late summer.
      The metal bridges, superstructures,
          black inkings,
    a carbon sketch we pass through,
    absorbent line, dark mass: impossible,
        bruised colors radiant around us.

There is great pain in not being beautiful,
in knowing what is beautiful, what is awesome,
in rendering poorly that which is of utterest beauty.

        We are not distressed by this now.
        We are calm, hovering,
    casting small shadow on the debate of
    is-it-all/is-it-nothing-at-all. There is no urgency,
        only great importance,

    the lights gathered around us,
    amber, warm as flesh,
        like islands, villages,
        themselves lighted with white lights.

We begin to sense this life
without weight,
        a life of meticulous care,
    our word full while empty, evanescent, absolute.

We are together, here,
driving over water on a black bridge,
differing angels, hair, wind, water,
hissing in flames.

❋ A Sighting of Whales

Irish moss thick on the coastal scrub
like a blossoming head of smoke,
the vast tilted crossings of road
and rocky meadow,
the patterns of tame animals—cow, horse, sheep.
Behind, the city in its chill mist and violet light.
Noon sun over all, white in the dense haze,
high clouding, slate-colored in part,
patches of bright uncolored sunlight
moving from the towers of business
to the bay across madrona grove and redwood,
farms and seal rocks, to the sea and the passages
of the sea and past the sea.
And this is the world as it is,
and our lesson is entry into it.

We watch in an odd kind of quiet,
lining cliffs and steps, the lighthouse rockery
and railings, staring to all sides, in pairs and trios,
some into the apocalyptic corridor of glare
where the colorless sun is sliding down its thread
to seawater in silver flame far below,
watching for the sudden spume,
the surfacing brow and back, the vast lift of tail,
perhaps for the special shock of their breaking,
a leap of one, two, three vast lives
in balletic series, rising for a moment
into the endless blur of light, water, warm air,
wind, into the feeling of connection and awe.

One blows, another nuzzling beside
a moment later, our fixed community suddenly stilled,

one or two pointing to the left of the brightest glare,
instructing others, palms to eyes—
then a break, a *leap*, electrical,
and all of us are applauding, shouting, in tears,
near blind with the day of waiting, with gratitude.

We are those who have waited,
ruined faith, broken eye,
alone in the terror of a natureless world,
seeking to know how to know, see how to see,
some bent to seedlings and moss,
others to the leviathan and its young
as they follow a warmth in the waters
toward the place they were born.

Seabirds lift and settle again, white among rocks,
lost in patterns of foam, winding lace-like
at stone footings.
The twin creatures show once again,
modestly, briefly, in the full, terrible glare
where the light makes of them dark silhouettes,
mottled, difficult to look at,
little more than a sense of large movement,
a double plume of spray.

✻

spring rain: young thin grass
under the eucalyptus
on the army base

❋ Pine/Eucalyptus/Fennel

Odors of the pine needle floor:
    the thin, dry smell of the upper pine inch,
the scent of the deeper plane of acrid mulch
    —both hung low, mixed, close to the ground
on which we lie, breathing.

    Eucalyptus leaves fallen onto this,
leather-like, flat, fragrant,
    the twisted wooden rags of bark,
      camphored, crossing with spiders' webs
    through tree shadow.

Beyond, an herb grove of fennel
at the head of the hill,
    dry in the green heat of this summer light.

    Sea-moist salt scent, bay water
blowing up the sand ridge,
cool tide, lap over lap,
      out of rhythm, clean as rain
    on the sweat of our bodies.

❋ Koi

The color of rose hip, persimmon,
papaya, coal and parchment;
the mixed colors of the nasturtium bed
in summer under the dark apple:
red-tossed, yellow-patched, tan-spattered,
banded black, blue, gray:
pool of koi, bodies turning slowly
in cool, shallow water, creatures not of depth
but of stillness, age, of retreat from havoc,
particolored angels of a muteness, seen, silent,
waiting in water until we return from gross business
with tea
to cease that business and bow
because the spirit needs sorely to surrender,
bow to their pond, to their place in the green-walled garden,
there to take us out of time.

At such times we are this:
the single apple leaf riding the surface
pushed by the mouthing of fish,
tumble of orange, yellow,
beige over tan.

✳ *Towards Sleep*

After words, acts: only details—
    the small head on the clavicle,
        right arm numb, the wrapped work of the heart,
  plush sounding.

        Night, uncertain throws of light,
        and the defiance of time in a human coupling
        that has rooted itself outside its own events.

We can come to hate the day for what it hides of us,
what little it shows.

        And at night, what is it that was hidden
        and is now revealed?

Nothing. Unseen light. Our own significance
in the pale glance of the quarter moon.

        Our thinness, this poverty
        isolated in a darkness of juniper,
        a balloon flower, opening in response
        to being seen at last, blue face upturned.

We are forever,
forever falling from the porch light
        through the autumn canes of rose,

the near-bare branches of apple,
onto the floor, in coin patterns,
onto this episode of skin,

where, leg crooked
over neck,
spine climbing up through hair, we pour,

sundial in the dark garden.

❋ Beach Walk

A harbor of round stones,
the hoods of crabs bright as sunset,
the color of flayed salmon flesh,
left in the sunlight where gulls have feasted
and gone,
green-white wands of sea oats arching fruit through wreckage,
alive in the yardage of cable rusting into knot and honeycomb,
seaweeds, the bone-wrack of fish, dried into a twisted language,
displayed with shell, small stone, chips of fraying wood
and yet nothing seems ever to happen; the beach is always
discovered with a quiet litter of events, enormous,
multiple, seemingly brief, always in the past.

To think that all this has occurred
in our lifetimes, yours and mine, in a series of days,
unnoticed before our eyes as we stared at each other, wary
of the past, careful of our futures,
focused by a human love,
our small hem of the tide . . . .

It is difficult to tell ourselves that we live as we live;
we need these sun-stretched days that harbor
us while we drift over our own evidence,
learning we are grateful, awe-filled, knowing we've been touched
by a finger of the wet wind and halted,
breathing with its whistle in the shell-like place
of our having lived together.

Photograph by Maz Livingston

Richard Ronan

A Radiance Like Wind or Water is Richard Ronan's sixth book of poetry, and his second for Dragon Gate, Inc. The poems in this collection reflect the author's lifelong interest in Zen and Japanese culture. An accomplished student of ikebana, he has also written a critical work on Bashō, the seventeenth century haiku poet, and has worked for several years rendering classical and contemporary haiku into English. Richard Ronan is a noted playwright as well, and has had a number of his theater pieces produced by avant-garde theater groups throughout the country. He currently lives and works in San Francisco.